IN FOCUS: NATIVE AMERICANS

COMANCHE

HISTORY AND CULTURE

MARK STEWART

Cavendish Square

Published in 2026 by Cavendish Square Publishing, LLC
2544 Clinton Street, Buffalo, NY 14224

Website: cavendishsq.com

Portions of this work were originally authored by David Lee and published as *Comanche* (Spotlight on Native Americans). All new material this edition authored by Mark Stewart.

Publisher: Katie Kawa
Book Design: Lisa Miley

Portions of this work were reviewed by: Robert J. Conley, Former Sequoyah Distinguished Professor at Western Carolina University and Director of Native American Studies at Morningside College and Montana State University.

Photo Credits: Library of Congress (5*, 13*, 15*, 19 both*); Sarony, Major & Knapp (6 top*); Tupungato/Shutterstock.com (6 bottom); University of California Libraries (7*); Frederic Remington (8*); Underwood Archives/Archive Photos/Getty Images (9); George Catlin/ Smithsonian American Art Museum (10*, 11 top*, 17*); DEA Picture Library/De Agostini/Getty Images (11 bottom); Theo Westenberger/ Hulton Archive/Getty Image (12); Carlisle Indian School Digital Resource Center (14); Frederic Lewis/Archive Photos/Getty Images; Alexander Gardner/National Archives (18*); U.S. Fish and Wildlife Service (20); Courtesy of North American Auction Co. (21); FA2010/ Wikimedia Commons (22); Courtesy of Cal State San Marcos (23 top); Author's Collection (23 bottom, 25); Charly Triballeau/AFP/Getty Images (24); J. Scott Applewhite/AP Images (26–27); Peter Turnley/Corbis/VCG via Getty Images (28); Comanche Nation Casino (29).

Cover images (clockwise from top): George Catlin/National Gallery of Art*; Peter Turnley/Corbis/VCG via Getty Images; Library of Congress*; Missouri History Museum*; Edward Curtis/Library of Congress*; Peter Turnley/Corbis/VCG via Getty Images.

*These images are in the public domain.

Cataloging-in-Publication Data
Names: Stewart, Mark, 1960 July 7-.
Title: Comanche history and culture / Mark Stewart.
Description: Buffalo, NY : Cavendish Square Publishing, 2026. | Series: In focus: Native Americans | Includes glossary and index.
Identifiers: ISBN 9781502674760 (pbk.) | ISBN 9781502674777 (library bound) | ISBN 9781502674784 (ebook)
Subjects: LCSH: Comanche Indians--Juvenile literature. | Comanche Indians--Social life and customs--Juvenile literature. | Indians of North America--Juvenile literature. | Indigenous peoples--Social life and customs--Juvenile literature.
Classification: LCC E99.C85 S94 2026 | DDC 978.004'974572--dc23

CPSIA compliance information: Batch #CS26CSQ: For further information contact Cavendish Square Publishing LLC at 1-877-980-4450.
Printed in the United States of America

CONTENTS

ABOUT OUR GLOSSARY

In this book, there may be several words or terms you are reading for the first time, or words that are familiar but used in an unusual way. All of these words appear in **bold type** throughout the book and are defined on page 30.

I AM THE LAND

One of the most unforgiving stretches of land in the American Southwest is called the Llano Estacado. The name is Spanish for "staked plain," referring to the tall wooden stakes that make up the walls of a frontier fort, or stockade. This vast, high desert region, located in northwest Texas and parts of New Mexico, was the heart of the territory claimed by the Comanche people. From this **imposing** natural fortress and the lands around it, the Comanches created an **empire** that held back invasions by three world powers—and became the most feared tribe in the Americas.

A Comanche warrior named Ako poses with his horse in a photograph from 1892.

Some think the Comanche name is of Spanish origin—*camino ancho*. This means "the broad trail," which refers to the wide paths worn in the desert during Comanche raids, which often involved 100 mounted warriors or more. Others think it comes from *komantsis* a Ute word that means "enemy." The Comanches call themselves "the people" or "people of people"—the word in their language is *nermernuh*.

◀ The Comanche people were masters of a harsh, imposing environment.

This illustration shows a Comanche creek-side settlement.

The Comanche people trace their roots to the Great Basin, a region west of the Rocky Mountains. They developed as a branch of the Eastern Shoshone tribe and for many centuries lived east of the Rockies as **nomadic** hunter-gatherers, in current-day Wyoming. The Comanche people did not have complex rituals or a **social structure**. They did not make pottery or baskets. Their scattered bands were focused on one thing: the daily fight for survival.

During the 1600s, the Comanches began moving south down the Great Plains, migrating through Colorado, Kansas, New Mexico, Oklahoma, and finally to Texas,

where they settled in a wide, flat area that covered hundreds of square miles and also includes the Palo Duro Canyon system—the second-largest in North America after the Grand Canyon.

Over the next 150 years, this part of the Southwest became known as the Comancheria. During that time, the Comanches defended their territory with a mix of intelligence and brutality that earned the fear and respect of anyone daring to oppose them. They also launched raids—often by moonlight—that stretched as far south as Mexico.

Before the Comanches migrated south, the Rocky Mountains were part of Shoshone territory.

People have been living in this region for more than 10,000 years. When the Comanches arrived, it was occupied by the Apache people. Both possessed great fighting skill and knowledge of the landscape, but Comanche warriors had something the Apaches did not—horses—and they pushed the Apaches west into the desert.

FIRST CONTACT

The first mention of the Comanche people in European writing dates back to 1706, from an account by a Spanish soldier in Taos, New Mexico. By then, the Comanches were already known as aggressive raiders who had mastered the art of hunting and fighting on horseback. The source of their horses was the Spanish, who had begun colonizing the region in the 1500s. In 1680, Spanish settlers were driven back into Mexico, leaving thousands of horses behind. By the time they returned 12 years later, the horse had transformed Comanche culture.

This painting shows the arrival of Spanish soldiers in the Southwest.

European military tactics had enabled Spanish **conquistadors** to subdue Indigenous people from South and Central America up into the Great Plains.

In 1858, the famous Texas Rangers turned their attention to fighting the Comanches.

However, even the most well-armed, well-trained soldiers were helpless against Comanche raids, which simply overwhelmed them. The horses bred and trained by Comanches were highly prized and were often traded for guns—which only increased the tribe's strength. With unmatched **mobility** and firepower, the tribe raided Spanish settlements at will throughout the 1700s—taking more horses and more weapons—and expanding their territory to more than 70,000 square miles (181,300 sq km), which is about the size of New England. The Comanches also halted efforts by the French to expand west from the territory around the Mississippi River.

The Comanches made an alliance with Spain in 1787, but that only lasted until Mexicans began fighting Spain for independence in the early 1800s. Comanches returned to their raiding and, in the years that followed, successfully defended themselves against forces from Mexico, the **Republic of Texas**, and the United States.

I AM A WARRIOR

The Comanche people lived for countless centuries in the mountainous regions of North America before migrating south. They looked a little different than the Great Plains tribes they encountered along the way. A Comanche warrior was likely to be short and square, with strong legs, a barrel chest, and massive shoulders. He could propel an arrow with enormous force and quickly overpower enemies in hand-to-hand combat. The Comanches studied their rivals like they studied the animals they hunted (such as bison), noting their habits and their weaknesses.

Although all Great Plains tribes acquired horses, no one **adapted** to them as quickly or as completely as the Comanches. They learned how to breed

This painting shows a Comanche warrior with a bow and shield.

In battle, Comanche warriors and their horses worked as one. Boys began their training soon after they could walk.

and train horses, and changed their fighting tactics to take full advantage of the horse. While other tribes used horses primarily as transportation to and from battle, the Comanches developed remarkable horsemanship that enabled them to fight without dismounting.

A Comanche boy was given his own horse as early as the age of four. He began his military training around age six and was an accomplished bareback rider by his teen years. Military training involved all of the skills needed to fight while galloping at full speed. A Comanche warrior could launch more than a dozen arrows in the time it took a soldier with a rifle to fire once and reload. They were deadly accurate at 100 feet (30 m)

or more. Another weapon that was effective while fighting on horseback was the Comanche lance. It measured 10 to 14 feet (3 to 4 m) and could be used against opponents on foot or on horseback. Comanche warriors usually took small shields into battle for protection.

The most important skill a Comanche warrior could learn was how to lower his body to one side of the horse while riding at full speed. This shielded him from enemy weapons. Warriors learned this by picking up objects on the ground at a full gallop—starting with small items and progressing to the point where they could pick up another warrior. Rescuing fallen comrades in this way was not done to become a hero. It was expected of every Comanche fighter.

The last great war chief of the Comanches was Quanah Parker. He was the son of a Comanche warrior and Cynthia Ann Parker, an American captured at the age of nine who became known as the "white squaw." As an adult, she so **embraced** tribal life that she refused on several occasions to return to her family in Texas. Quanah was young, fearless, and clever.

◀ Comanche performers demonstrate the Comanche Shield Dance—which symbolizes a conflict over territory—at the American Indian Dance Theater in New York City.

A NEW REALITY

The Comanches were the unchallenged masters of the Great Plains for more than 150 years. Their horsemanship and fighting skills enabled them to control bison herds—the region's most important source of food—over thousands of square miles. During the 1850s and 1860s, the United States set a goal of connecting east and west. Native tribes in the "path of progress" were relocated from their homes to reservation lands. Those that did not go willingly were subdued in battle.

The Comanches signed a treaty with the U.S. in 1867 agreeing to move to reservation land. However, many refused to yield. They outfought and outsmarted U.S. troops at almost every turn. President Ulysses S. Grant, who had seen what it took to defeat a determined enemy as a general during the Civil

◀ Solomon Chandler, shown at the Carlisle Indian School, was one of many Comanche children sent to special government boarding schools in the 1880s and 1890s.

This photo shows the generals appointed by President Grant to fight the Comanches following the Civil War.

War, made victory over the Comanches a top priority. The Army sent thousands of experienced, mounted soldiers to fight them. They were armed with new rapid-firing weapons, including the Colt **revolver** and an early version of the machine gun.

The U.S. government also encouraged destruction of the bison herds to cut off the Comanches' food supply. During the winter of 1874–75, the Comanche people were cold and starving. They were removed to a reservation in Oklahoma, where they were forced to become farmers on land that was not very fertile. Many of their children were made to attend boarding schools that stripped them of their culture and traditions. Adjusting to reservation life went against almost every aspect of Comanche culture.

BEING COMANCHE

During their time as masters of the Comancheria, the Comanche people divided themselves into tribal units that occupied different territory and operated independently. By the mid-1800s, they had six divisions: Kwahada (antelope), Penatekas (honey eaters), Tenewa (downstream people), Nokoni (wanderers), Kotsotekas (buffalo eaters), and Yamparika (root eaters). All of these groups depended heavily on the bison herds the tribe controlled.

The central focus of Comanche life was the horse. Every man, woman, and child was expected to become an expert rider, breeder, and trainer of horses. Although women were not expected to fight on horseback, they were able to do so if their village came under attack. They also used horses to hunt; there is a famous description

Comanche tribal units occupied different areas and operated independently.

This painting shows a Comanche village during the 1830s. Every man, woman, and child was capable of fighting off attacks.

of two Comanche women working together to rope an antelope, which shows what skilled riders they were.

The amount of time young women spent on horseback may have contributed to a problem the Comanches experienced: low fertility. This term refers to when a population has fewer children than it should, compared to its overall size. One way the Comanches addressed this challenge was by taking young children captive during their raids and then raising them as Comanches.

The Comanche people lived a nomadic lifestyle. They followed the seasons and the bison herds, living in tipis (tepees) that could be quickly set up and taken down when a village had to move. This was an important

responsibility of women in Comanche culture; tipis were the property of women, not men. Women collected wild plants for food and medicine, passing this knowledge down to their daughters. Comanche women also **processed** animal hides into clothing and robes. The trading of bison robes was an important part of the tribe's economy.

Bison provided for almost all the Comanches' needs, from bowstrings to glue. Bison meat provided fresh food and could also be preserved and stored for winter food or trail food. Comanches cut the meat into thin strips, salted it, and hung it in the sun to make dried meat that would last a long time.

▲ A Comanche medicine man poses for a photo in the 1890s.

Horses were a measure of status and wealth. A Comanche chief might have 1,000 horses. A chief in another Great Plains tribe might have 50. The Comanche language also showed how important horses were. While their vocabulary was very basic, the words they used to describe the color and appearance of different horses numbered in the dozens.

◀ Comanche women were in charge of their family's tipi and processed bison hides that were important trade items.

SOMETHING SACRED

The origin story of the Comanche people tells of a time when great swirling winds from the four directions kicked up dust in a giant storm. The wind created people with the power of storms and the strength of the earth from which they had been made. Comanche spiritual life was closely linked to their environment, as well as a very personal connection to the spirit world. The strength of this connection enabled someone to use his or her personal power, or *puha*, to become an effective healer or hunter or warrior—or whatever else they wanted to be. In this sense, the Comanches did not have a religious structure like many other tribes. However, they passed down their cultural traditions and beliefs through storytelling that featured

The coyote was an important animal in Comanche culture.

characters such as the Trickster Coyote, a mischievous animal with special powers.

Coyotes were important animals in Comanche culture. They watched the animal's behavior closely, believing that it had the ability to alert them about events in the future, both good and bad. Comanches never harmed a coyote and sometimes changed their plans when they saw one howling or barking. In many stories, coyotes were also forces of creativity and art.

Most examples of Comanche art that have survived from the time before the tribe was forced off its homeland are in museums or private collections. Many were taken from the tribe in the 1800s without their permission. Comanches were celebrated for their parfleches, which are finely crafted containers made of tanned elk hide. They are colored with natural dyes and decorated with beadwork and porcupine quills.

▲ Comanche beadwork from the 1800s, like this riding quirt—a type of short whip—are highly prized by collectors.

Today, the Comanche creative tradition is celebrated in the work of many artists, writers, and actors. For example, the bold, colorful paintings of Eric Tippeconnic are on exhibit in **galleries** and museums around the United States. He combines themes from his time growing up on Comanche reservations with influences from his mother's home country in Denmark.

Juanita Pahdopony is a celebrated Comanche poet, writer, and artist. Another Comanche writer, Cornel Pewewardy, has been a leading voice in the

This Comanche headdress from the 1880s is on display in a museum in Germany.

Artist Eric Tippeconnic draws on themes from his childhood on Comanche reservations.

effort to convince sports teams to abandon their Native American names and mascots.

Paul Chaat Smith, a Comanche-Choctaw whose parents were educators, has spent more than 20 years as a curator at the National Museum of the American Indian. He also wrote the humorous-but-informative book *Everything You Know About Indians Is Wrong*.

Perhaps the most recognizable artist of Comanche heritage is Gil Birmingham, an actor who has appeared in more than 50 films and television shows, including the popular *Twilight* series.

PAST, PRESENT, FUTURE

The United State government did not uphold many of the promises made to the Comanches after they agreed to move on to reservations. Without bison to **sustain** them, the tribe relied on food deliveries that often were inadequate or did not come at all. In the 1890s, a law was passed that split Native American reservation land into individual **parcels**. For a nomadic people that did not recognize land ownership, this was a major blow. It also led to a sale of "unoccupied" parcels to white settlers in the early 1900s. The original Comanche reservations got smaller and smaller. Slowly but surely, their identity was being erased and, with it, many of their traditions.

Preserving Comanche traditions for young people is an important goal of older tribal members.

This Comanche Nation patch celebrates the tribe's great heritage.

In 1934, the U.S. government cleared the way for the Comanches to officially join the Kiowa and Kiowa-Apache people. The Kiowa had often been allies of the Comanches when they lived on the southern Great Plains. During the 1960s, the Comanches broke away from this group and formed their own nation.

In the 2020 U.S. **census**, more than 28,000 people identified themselves as Comanche. About 17,000 of them are enrolled in the Comanche Nation and around 7,000 live on former reservation land that is under tribal control—most near the Oklahoma towns of Lawton and Fort Sill, where many work. The tribe provides healthcare and other services for its members, but rates of

CIVA
Comanche

unemployment, poverty, and addiction are still very high.

Tourism is another important part of the economy. The Comanche Museum and Cultural Center in Lawton has a wonderful collection of tribal artifacts. The town also plays host to the annual Comanche Nation Fair, which includes a traditional **powwow** and other events. It takes place each autumn and draws thousands of Comanche and non-Comanche visitors. It is the largest Native American gathering in the region.

◀ In 2013, Comanches were part of a Congressional Gold Medal ceremony in Washington, D.C. The tribe was recognized for its wartime contributions.

Drawing attention to Comanche life and history also helps to protect the Comanche language, which is in danger of disappearing. It is one of the oldest languages in the Americas, but the number of fluent speakers in **dwindling**. The challenge faced by the Comanches and other tribes is finding positive strategies for blending modern life and traditional customs in ways that engage their young people and inspire them to preserve their language and culture.

A major source of revenue for the Comanche Nation comes from the many casinos and hotels that it currently operates. They are popular destinations located roughly midway between the cities of Dallas, Texas, and Oklahoma City, Oklahoma.

◀ Hard-working Wallace Coffey is pictured in 1992, the year he became chairman of the Comanche Nation. He served six terms before retiring in 2016 and became the "face" of the Comanche people during that time.

GLOSSARY AND FURTHER READING

GLOSSARY

Adapted—Adjusted in response to new opportunities or conditions.

Census—A government count that takes place every 10 years.

Conquistadors—A Spanish soldier or "conqueror" of the 1500s and 1600s.

Dwindling—Gradually shrinking in size.

Embraced—Accepted with great enthusiasm.

Empire—A great amount of territory controlled by one group or person.

Galleries—Businesses that exhibit and promote the work of artists.

Imposing—On a grand scale.

Mobility—The ability to move freely and easily.

Nomadic—Moving from place to place.

Parcels—Units of land that can be bought and sold.

Powwow— A large Native American ceremony or celebration.

Processed—Performed a series of steps to change or preserve something.

Republic of Texas—An independent nation that existed in current-day Texas between 1836 and 1846.

Revolver—A pistol that can be fired several times without reloading.

Social Structure—A set of organized rules and relationships that guide the way people behave within a group.

Sustain—Strengthen or support.

BOOKS

Krupat, Arnold. *Boarding School Voices: Carlisle Indian School Students Speak*. Lincoln, NE: University of Nebraska Press, 2021.

Rossiter, Brienna. *The Trail of Tears*. Mendota Heights, MN: North Star Editions, 2025.

Tyler, Ron. *Native Americans: The Complete Plates of McKenney, Catlin, and Bodmer*. Cologne, Germany: Taschen America, 2024.

Various Authors. *My Life: Growing Up Native in America*. New York, NY: MTV Books/Simon & Schuster Children's Publishing, 2024.

ABOUT THE AUTHOR

MARK STEWART has written more than 150 non-fiction books for educational publishers, covering history, sports, and popular culture. His family tree tells a complex story common to many Americans. Mark's ancestors include some of the first European colonists, as well as the Indigenous people with whom early settlers interacted. Some faced off on the field of battle while others fought side-by-side. His 10th great-grandfather was **Myles Standish**, an officer on the ***Mayflower***, while his ninth great-grandmother was **Singing Bird Corbison**, who was described as a "Shawnee woman" but who was probably from the **Wampanoag** tribe. The Wampanoag people saved Standish and his fellow **Pilgrims** from starvation during the winter of 1620–21, forming the basis for the story of Thanksgiving. The descendants of Corbison and Standish blended into a single family in 1789, and then headed west in search of opportunity. This brought Mark's ancestors into direct conflict with Native people along the frontier in the 1700s and 1800s. Mark's sixth great-grandmother recalled frantically casting bullets for her husband as they defended their small Kentucky fort from an attack. Another served under 23-year-old **Abraham Lincoln** in the Illinois Militia during the Black Hawk War of 1832. Mark's more recent ancestors chose to fight their battles with words—as writers and editors of books, newspapers, and magazines. In 2007, he authored a history of the **Indian Removal Act of 1830** and the infamous **Trail of Tears**.

INDEX